HELLO, I'M JADYN!

LEARNING ABOUT MAKING FRIENDS

Katherine Eason

FOX EYE
PUBLISHING

Jadyn wanted to make new friends.
But he felt too **SHY** to say hello.

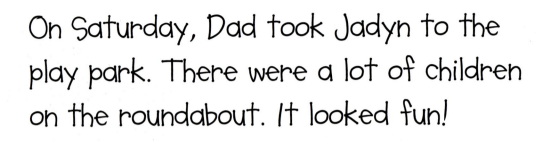

On Saturday, Dad took Jadyn to the play park. There were a lot of children on the roundabout. It looked fun!

Jadyn saw a boy from his class.
The boy asked Jadyn if he wanted to play on the swings.

Jadyn didn't **SPEAK**. He felt too **SHY**. He just hid behind Dad.

The next day, Dad and Jadyn went to the swimming pool. Jadyn saw his neighbour, Emily.

At school, a new boy called Oliver joined the class. Miss Book told Oliver to sit next to Jadyn. Oliver smiled at Jadyn.

At lunchtime, Jadyn sat on his own.
Oliver sat at the same table.
They both ate their lunch.

But they didn't **SPEAK** to each other.

At home, Jadyn told Dad what had happened at school. Dad said that a lot of people are shy, and that's OK. Dad said that he felt shy as a boy, too. Then Dad asked Jadyn if he thought Oliver was **LONELY**. What if Oliver was **SHY**, too?

Jadyn thought about it. Maybe it was important to **MAKE FRIENDS** with Oliver.

The next day, Jadyn **SAID HELLO** to Oliver. Jadyn said that he liked swimming. Oliver said that he did too. Jadyn and Oliver sat together at lunchtime. They both smiled.

Jadyn **FELT HAPPY**. He had learnt to **MANAGE FEELING SHY** and had **MADE A NEW FRIEND**.

Words and Behaviour

Jadyn was too shy to make new friends in this story and that caused a lot of problems.

There are a lot of words to do with making new friends in this book. Can you remember all of them?

SHY

MAKE FRIENDS

JOIN IN

Let's talk about feelings and manners

This series helps children to understand difficult emotions and behaviours and how to manage them. The characters in the series have been created to show emotions and behaviours that are often seen in young children, and which can be difficult to manage.

Hello, I'm Jadyn!

The story in this book examines the reasons for making friends. It looks at why making new friends is important and how making friends stops people from feeling lonely and helps them to join in.

How to use this book

You can read this book with one child or a group of children. The book can be used to begin a discussion around complex behaviour such as making friends.

The book is also a reading aid, with enlarged and repeated words to help children to develop their reading skills.

How to read the story

Before beginning the story, ensure that the children you are reading to are relaxed and focused.

Take time to look at the enlarged words and the illustrations, and discuss what this book might be about before reading the story.

New words can be tricky for young children to approach. Sounding them out first, slowly and repeatedly, can help children to learn the words and become familiar with them.

How to discuss the story

When you have finished reading the story, use these questions and discussion points to examine the theme of the story with children and explore the emotions and behaviour within it:

- What do you think the story was about?
- Have you been in a situation in which you found it difficult to make new friends? What was that situation?
- Do you think making new friends doesn't matter? Why?
- Do you think making new friends is important? Why?
- What could go wrong if you don't make any friends?

Titles in the series

    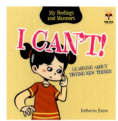

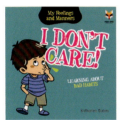 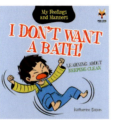   

   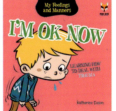 

First published in 2023 by Fox Eye Publishing
Unit 31, Vulcan House Business Centre,
Vulcan Road, Leicester, LE5 3EF
www.foxeyepublishing.com

Copyright © 2023 Fox Eye Publishing
All rights reserved. No portion of this book may be
reproduced in any form without permission from the
publisher, except as permitted by U.K. copyright law.

Author: Katherine Eason
Art director: Paul Phillips
Cover designer: Emma Bailey
Editor: Jenny Rush

All illustrations by Novel

ISBN 978-1-80445-176-2

Printed in China